Also by William Trowbridge

Father and Son (Wayne State College Press) 2024.

Call Me Fool (Red Hen Press) 2022.

Oldguy: Superhero—The Complete Collection
(Red Hen Press) 2019.

Vanishing Point (Red Hen Press) 2017.

Put This On, Please: New & Selected Poems
(Red Hen Press) 2014.

Ship of Fool (Red Hen Press) 2011.

The Complete Book of Kong (Southeast Missouri
State University Press) 2003.

Flickers (University of Arkansas Press) 2000.

O Paradise (University of Arkansas Press) 1995.

Enter Dark Stranger (University of Arkansas Press) 1989.

MAINTENANCE

Poems by William Trowbridge

Spartan
Press

Spartan Press
Kansas City, MO
spartanpresskc@gmail.com

Spartan
Press

Copyright © William Trowbridge, 2025
First Edition: 1 3 5 7 9 10 8 6 4 2
ISBN: 979-8-89975-016-8
LCCN: 2025940843

Author photo: Hank Young
Cover image: *Powerhouse Mechanic*, Lewis W. Hine, 1920

Acknowledgments:

American Journal of Poetry—"Maintenance," "Going Native."

Birmingham Poetry Review—"Lucky Them," "Six to Ten Inches," "Voyage to Outer Space."

Black Renaissance Noir—"Committee Meeting," "Moon."

Chariton Review—"After Surprising Conversions."

Gasconade Review—"Autumn House Express," "Back Then," "Teaching Shakespeare."

Green Hills Literary Lantern—"At Military School," "Captain Video, 1952."

Green Mountains Review—""Shoe," "Snipe Hunt.

I-70 Review—"Over Our Head," "Doubters Gate," "Cash Cow," "At Long Last."

New Letters—"Contagion," "Speed."

Plume—"Post Mortem," "On Bruegel's *Massacre of the Innocents*," "A Second Look at Bruegel's *The Tower of Babel*," "Viva Villa," "Harvard Classics," "Mr. Bissell," "Little Known Royal Cognomens."

Rattle—"Song of the Black Hole," "Family Album."

Rosebud— 'Redeye Pins."

Salt—"I didn't Know," "Scouting," "Now You See It, Now You don't," "Don't Ask."

South Dakota Review—"Hot Spell," "Invasion."

Tar River Poetry— "Lament for the Hot Rods."

Thorny Locust—"Baccalaureate," "Apostasy," "Dulce et Decorum."

Undocumented: Great Lakes Poets Laureate on Social Justice, eds. Ronald Riekki and Andrea Scarpino, Michigan State University Press, East Lansing, MI, 2019—"Mercy."

Verse Viral— "Archaeopteryx," "Radiation Day."

World Literature Today—"The Ones Who'd Carry it Out."

TABLE OF CONTENTS

I

II

III

IV

For Sue,
wife and partner though the years.

MAINTENANCE

I

BACK THEN

when time was just there, like the air you breathed,
when hardship was Algebra II,
when work was over at the 3:15 bell,
when you could put a little balm on it and run it off,
when fear was the grade card that could get you grounded,
when death was getting grounded,
when torture was an hour in old Miss Harper's Bible class,
when freedom from oppression was a driver's license,
when courage was buying a six-pack with a phony I.D.,
when disaster was getting caught using a phony I.D.,
when true love was eternal, like everything but Grandpa.

DON'T ASK

I got it for my seventh birthday, football
from a Missouri/Kansas game, bearing
scuffs from the hands and feet of heroes
I'd only seen in photos. It nearly glowed.

My neighborhood pals admired it as we
scrimmaged in the back yard, feeling
its leathery heft. I even let Tommy Nash,
outsider from down the street, join in.

Next morning, in the place I'd left it
on our screened-in porch, the ball
bore five stab marks beneath the laces
and what looked like half a footprint.

A few days prior, Tommy'd showed off
his new pocket knife, its bone handle
and shiny blade, how well it fit the hand.
He said we could look but not touch.

It seemed unreal: my new football,
its sturdy hide, its elegance, flattened
on the porch like road-kill. Why?

NOW YOU SEE IT, NOW YOU DON'T

said Al the Marvelous to our third-grade class
as his droop-eared rabbit disappeared. We clapped
at its return. That very year, when Miss Fisher

told us Al had "passed away," I thought he might
wave himself back with a whoosh of his wrinkly cape—
not like Grandpa, who went into the sky to stay with God.

In my father's novelty catalog, I discovered The Magic
Wand Outfit, which offered "many marvelous mystifying
wonders of wizardry," perhaps the secret of the rabbit

or even the whereabouts of Al. Better, I thought,
The Magician's Ring, "in great favor throughout
the conjuring fraternity," might summon him.

But Al and the marvels faded fast when I turned
to the ("Watch them jump!") Joy Buzzer, which I hoped
would make that bully Gerald Dudik disappear.

CYCLIST

I ride a Monark, 26-inch rims,
maroon, with yellow trim. Where
motorcycle gas would be, there's

a tank with batteries and a button
for the horn. My handlebars have
green and yellow streamers. Girls have

24-inch rims, and no straddle bar,
which could lift dresses into the wind
and show their panties. If I get

a flat, I can patch the inner-tube.
I can lubricate the chain and axles.
I can ride no-hands for a block and do

suicide spins on slippery spots. I keep
my bike washed and chamoised, buff
with Simoniz. My buddies all have

26-inch rims. In a year or so, when
we get 28s, we'll be ready to ride like
the 7th graders, clear past 49th street.

APOSTASY

If this is the way to celebrate the flight from Egypt,
I'd rather go back.
                    —Michael Blumenthal on a Passover Seder

Alan Epstein, my fourth-grade best buddy
in our crowd that practiced cap-gun war
and hook slides, cherry-bomb dares and

Scout-camp demerit earning, struggled
to escape from beneath the yoke of the faith
he was born into: Hebrew school after school,

when *The Lone Ranger* and *Superman* were on,
and on Saturdays, the day-long Shabbat
with his sternly orthodox parents, feeding

matzo, challah, cholent, instead of pizza,
Kool-Aid, Popsicles; prayer instead of
bike riding, Monopoly, kick the can.

"Kikes," he called his parents and their friends.
Christmas trees were "hanukah bushes,"
their rabbi, a "Hebe." It's been 70 years

since I last saw him, but I think of him
now and then, enmeshed in that early form
of spirit versus appetite, which my family's

vaguely Protestant leanings excused me from.
I hope he grew to find balance enough to make
his later life, in the ecumenical sense, kosher.

THE ALLEY KIDS

Mother told me to come in when they
appeared, shaggy among hollyhocks

that grew thick as jungle verdure
behind our backyard—Indian territory,

the other side of the DMZ, sheer drop
off the edge of our squared little planet.

They were all related, the story went,
spawned from some woolly gene pool,

nearly interchangeable. The meanest
had a club foot and once punched me

breathless after school. Why were they
so hurtful? Dad said they had nothing

else to do. They needed a good, hard
scrubbing, a lesson in right manners,

shop class. Then they could slough off
alley ways, go out for sports. Play ball.

THE WOUNDS OF TOM MIX

(on the back of a Ralston cereal box)

With Xs to mark fractures and Os
for bullet holes, some alone and some
in clusters, this cowboy's silhouette outdid
the direst renderings of Saint Sebastian:
A. Skull fractured in an accident; B. Nose
injured when artillery wagon blew up
in China, C. Apache arrow wound (and
close call for his mythic manhood),
and on through Z—twenty-six
stigmata for us Straight Shooters,

sworn to the official oath, official
view that "Lawbreakers always lose,
Straight Shooters always win! It pays
to shoot straight!!!" Doubters could
touch the ring, decoder badge; believers
follow the trail of saintliness his horse
dropped along the airwaves, amid news
of Uncle Sam and Rinso White,
rumors of Katyn and Buchenwald.

CAPTAIN VIDEO, 1952

After school, it thundered in on Wagner's
"Flying Dutchman Overture." OK, maybe

it sputtered some on 25-bucks-a-week,
the Captain and the Video Ranger wearing

ski goggles on painted football helmets
to battle histrionic villains on cloth planets.

But so what if Mars was a drawing
on a canvas flat, also Venus, Neptune

et. al. And who cared that controls
on the Captain's ship, *Galaxy II*, featured

a TV screen small as ours, a lever,
and several wheels, all on another flat,

that a midway filler flipped to oater serials:
Riders of Death Valley, Deadwood Dick,

or that our Captain wound up demoted
to dentist in a toothpaste ad and his Ranger

from cosmic duty to daytime soaps.
On the *Galaxy's* interrupted flights, I swear

we conquered space. And saved the earth.
I remember. I was there.

POLIO DAYS

In 1949, the War had all but vanished
from *Life*, diffusing to a pale gray dream
that drifted in from across the ocean.
There was a cold war now, and polio
roamed the neighborhoods. I learned
the Duck and Cover drill and filled
slots in our March of Dimes card;
Mother scrubbed peaches till they bled.

My G.I. father fought to run a packing house,
a giant furnace stoked with cows and pigs.
As pigs bled out, they screamed like humans.
I thought that if I fell into the scalding tank
my skin would slip off easy as my snowsuit.
Pig heads dangling on hooks nodded yes.

My father's snouted .45 fired rounds
big as a grown man's little finger. "Never
clean it till you check the chamber," he said,
telling of a sadsack who took bullet
and cleaning rod through the skull. "Little hole
here," he said, touching my forehead,
"and the rest on the barracks wall."

He brought it in the car, cocked on the seat,
to picket lines of angry Poles and Czechs.
"They killed a scab," he told Mother, "bombed
his house." In *Life's Picture History*

of World War II, a London tot, mouth open,
stared up at Hitler's black planes. I learned
polio is also called "infantile paralysis."

The night my father and I saw *Battleground*
at the Paramount, I woke to pigs screaming.
It was him, pinned down by his dream. "They're
still in my head," I heard him tell Mother.
I went home one day from playing Soldiers
to rest on the couch, where a chambered round
ignited my brain. I felt my skin slip loose.
The doctor said, "Try to touch your chest
with your chin." In an iron lung
only your head showed.

SCOUTING

La France bluing. . .whitens clothes,
saves time and labor.

—1955 magazine ad

By a narrow creek on a Scout hike
through woods outside Omaha,
we discovered a small blue box,

partly crushed in a pile of trash
somebody dumped there. All we
could make out was the label,

"La France," plus an instruction: "use
with soap." "Man, a box of rubbers!"
my pal Barry announced." You ever

seen anything else with a name
like that? Like in 'French kiss,' 'French
Tickler?'" There it was, no doubt,

what we'd heard about but never
seen, a trace of flesh's merit badge,
though the box had been used,

maybe had cast-off rubbers inside,
maybe alive with v.d. There was
nothing else to say or do about

what lay there in the wilderness. We hiked
on our way, lost in thought, anxious
to revisit our Playmate of the Month.

SNIPE HUNT

On a night campout, two old Scouts,
junior high age, handed us Tenderfeet
sticks and gunny sacks and sent us
into the woods to hunt for snipes,

which they said, smirking, were winged
and sounded like piccolos. We took it
as our mission, like those who sought
the Northwest Passage or Machu Picchu.

Could snipes be tamed? Would we win
a special merit badge? Instead, we got
mosquitoes and the scorch of poison ivy,
plus a chilly douse of old-boy yocks—

our welcome to the club that failed to find
the bacon stretcher, soufflé pump, skyhook,
striped paint, and K9P spray. Let that be
a lesson, our parents said, who'd learned

to trust in what they had: the mortgage,
faded sedan, steady work, pre-paid plots.
So we mowed the lawn, washed the car,
wrote our book reports on *Silas Marner*.

But after bed sometimes, we'd hear—
past our row of streetlights—snipes,
thronging skyward, moon-dappled,
piping their extravagant song.

GOING NATIVE

My parents feared my newfound scruffy pals
across the sea of 64th Street, the sullen,
unshorn ones whose parents scrapped like the cats
that lived inside a pickup hulk rusting
in their yard. "They could have impetigo,"
Mother said, "which doctors say can spread."

Their older brothers raised the bars on Hogs,
put megaphones where mufflers should have been,
tore wavy ruts across the football field—
suborned, intoned our pastor, by Rock 'n' Roll,
its tom-toms, too-low jeans, *(and you-know-what)*.

I let my crew-cut grow, my jeans hang down,
tried to speak their lingo, learn to dance
the Dirty Chicken, inked on a death's head, but
let Mother wash my clothes and make my bed.

I DIDN'T KNOW

that zits and braces were just for starters.

that bald-in-back Miss Harper's Bible class,
in "Fellowship Hall," which smelled of
mildew and stale tomato sauce, would be
like water torture you had to dress up for.

that for "choose partners" at the 7th-grade dance,
I'd get stuck, due to shyness, with the last girl
unchosen, forlorn in her muumuu smock
and extra chin, who probably considered me,
the guy with zits and a mouthful of hardware,
the last boy she'd want to get stuck with,
and who, after losing weight, would become
class beauty and walk right through me.

that the "X-ray" glasses I ordered off the back
of my Batman comic book couldn't see bras
or panties, much less what was underneath.

that my Clearasil, pinkish cream that cracked
on my face like dried mud and which I tried
to apply thinly enough to be invisible,
would bullhorn, "Look, everybody: leper!"

that our geography teacher would announce,
on the first day of class, that he liked to say
"Yucca Flat," liked nothing better than saying

"Yucca Flat," that whenever anyone would
provide him the opportunity to say "Yucca Flat"
— for instance, by asking him to name a nuclear
bomb-test site or a place near Frenchman's Flat —
he would greatly appreciate it.

that after I thought I nailed my audition for
a lead in our class play, *Blythe Spirit*, co-starring
the former fat girl, who might finally acknowledge
my existence, I'd land "other voice offstage."

that on the football team, whom coach Marvin
"Duke" Conroy required to practice in 100-degree
August weather, with no water allowed because it
might get us "water-logged" so we'd slosh through
the wind sprints and jumping jacks like clowns
in leaky waders, that I'd sub for the block--and-
tackle dummy.

that cheerleader Betty Sanders, whose high kicks,
bounces, twirls, cartwheels and saucy grin
got me goo-goo-eyed, would be caught
topless with coach Duke in the equipment locker.

that my Eagle Scout uniform, with its sashful
of merit badges and military press, would be taken
by classmates for a sad clown outfit and that
the Twelve Scout Virtues, which Scoutmaster
retired Marine Gunnery Sergeant Harold "Dog"
Davis had me speed-recite ten times while

standing at attention because my shoes weren't
shined enough, were composed especially
for block-and-tackle dummies.

INVASION

Omaha, January, 1958

Watch the skies, everywhere, keep looking!
Keep watching the skies!
    —The Thing from Another World

We heard it on the PA, second period:
three bodies found in a shack in Lincoln,
a couple and their daughter, age two, shot,

it seemed, by the older daughter's boyfriend,
Charles Starkweather, the child's body
stuffed into an outdoor privy. Another murder

was announced after math, and two more
during study hall, the killer and the girlfriend
said to be heading up toward us. What

could they want? There was an APB.
Radios chattered like we'd imagined
if the Russians finally struck, when the EBS

would tell us, "This is not a drill,"
as SAC bombers, kept ready out at Offutt,
lifted into WWIII. In Lincoln, the police chief

told citizens, "Arm yourselves!" like in *Invasion
of the Body Snatchers*, parkaed vigilantes
in the backs of pickups, prowling neighborhoods

for aliens. We imagined Starkweather's eyes
—unearthly, staring above a .38 or 12 gauge. What
would we do? We were frightened and light-hearted

as the teens who sounded the early warning
in *The Blob*. Our parents came to drive us home,
cars lining the street beside our high school.

We heard sirens on 72nd, saw police,
weapons drawn, storm Ryan's Junk Yard
on a false tip. But maybe he *had* arrived,

a thought that caromed through the state,
where the couple was seen in five towns
simultaneously. We felt surrounded. Mother,

eyes raised, asked God if anyone was safe
anymore. Dad loaded up his service .45
and scanned the TV news. "Duck and cover"

couldn't have saved those kids from Bennet,
found dumped in a storm cellar,
or the human noshes in *Night of the Living Dead*.

Three more dead, back in Lincoln,
said the news, as I watched cars pass our house,
one with a couple in it, moving slow. Too slow.

Nothing happened. A few days later,
they were caught: Starkweather, ex-garbageman,
stubby and bow-legged, who tried to comb his hair

like James Dean's, and his mousy girlfriend,
Caril Ann, 14, in cowgirl boots, who swore
she'd been a hostage. They looked haggard,

unexceptional, had surrendered meekly.
Life went back to normal: routine, secure.
Undeceived, we continued keeping watch.

MR. BISSELL

He's probably dead by now, like some of us.
A homely man who suffered from excessive
sweating, he taught us high school algebra.

By seventh hour, fall or spring, his brow
looked like a standup's whose best joke just died;
his crisp white shirt reshaped to sticky-limp,

with mustard yellow stains beneath the arms.
 We joked that his sweat emulsified with dust
from the yellow chalk he used, that you could smell

him from the third row. He must have loved
mathematics, its lucid certainty and grace,
its universe so self-contained, so free

from ridicule, loved it dearly enough
to suffer the daily trial of whispers, smirks,
and rolling eyes; of hallway cracks about

opening windows or running for the Air Wick.
His only smile was in his yearbook photo,
below it: "Virtue is its own reward."

I imagined he spent his hours after school
before a second-hand TV, eating
his TV dinner, a fan on "high," then off

to a lonely bed where the AC hummed him to
a clammy sleep. But maybe he had a wife
who'd have made our beauties look like crones,

the two of them sweating into meta-sex
after shots of vintage Scotch and slurps
of blue-point oysters—laughing now and then

about those squirmy pups he has to tame.
He'd earned no less, though it probably was his lot
to settle for a cry on virtue's chilly breast.

SPEED

If you don't crash now and then,
you don't know how fast you can go.
—Dave Aldana, Motorcycle Hall of Fame

It drew Bandini and von Trips
to kingdom come at Monza and Monaco,
and Vuckovich at Indy, and my high school pals

into a mountain outside Denver (morticians
couldn't tell whose parts were whose).
Speed—the pull of it, the blur, the white,

white rush inside that pocket of velocity,
where past and future plume off behind
like shreds of that contract

with your better brain as you hurtle
toward the vanishing point. And, yes,
that Brit, Moss, had it right: it's the curves,

not the straightaways, "having a bloody go"
at the "absolute limit of tyre adhesion,"
eyes, brain, muscle pressed into the arc,

like a painter stroking the perfect line,
like a safecracker when the tumblers click.
Like a stray soul plunged into bright water

and delivered: Jesus!

26

UNCONDITIONAL ELECTION
AND REPROBATION

is the Calvinist mouthful meaning God picked
the damned and saved before the Creation,
that the fix is in, no matter how hard you try

or don't to make Him like you. Some took that
to mean the richer you are the more likely
you're a lucky saint, that wealth signifies

God's holy nod. The rumor spread. Hence,
our church, Heartland Presbyterian, where
the moneyed worshipped, if they weren't Jews

or Catholics, where the altar featured "The Last
Supper," carved in cherry and brought from Italy
"at great expense," where my father dragged us

every Sunday to rub assets with the fat cats.
In Sunday school, old Mrs. Bradley told us
of the Good Samaritan and others, of their sad,

grubby necks beneath the feet of tyrants.
She said their like would inherit the earth,
to which our elders would have mouthed," Amen."

Mrs. Bradley, whose husband left her bankrupt,
had to move. "Poor soul," Mother said,
"doomed to that God-forsaken part of town."

II

ACROSS THE BORDER

I was raised in the suburbs of West Omaha,
where being a snot-nosed pantywaist
was a sign of proper upbringing. I finally
got a decent-paying job in South Omaha,
my junior year, where the sign was being

a switchblade-toting badass. Early mornings
on my way to work at Cudahy Packing,
I'd drive past the White Eagle Bar,
where, once a week, I'd see an ambulance,
red light flashing as they gantried out

the latest casualty, face milky, blood
soaking through the sheet. My workmates,
mostly Slavs—Dabrowski, Jankovic,
Kopecky—from Chicago via loss of goods
and home in WWII, told pussy jokes,

stretched breaks, and stole pork loins
off the line for lunch, cooking
them on the overhead steam pipes
that fed the knife sterilizers. They
foraged, something explorers did

in the jungle books I liked to read,
what Dabrowski did when home

was just a safe spot in the forest.
I got a month of non-stop razzing,
oil sprayed on my shoes, grimy
fat chunks left at my work station.
Finally, when I matched chunk for chunk,
they accepted me, a schoolboy fresh
from "Kanada," old-world name
for land of plenty. By summer's end,

I'd learned to forage a meal, game
high-handed bosses, hone a blade,
and speak the native dialect, which might
as well be known as "Fuck"—a tongue
not taught at Westside High.

SUMMER JOB

United Steel Workers,
Continental Can Co., Chicago

"You that newboy?"asked the guy
assigned to break me in, grizzled lifer
with Local 47 on his cap. "Emergency
stop," he said, nodding at a scarlet button
big as a Caddy hubcap, as we mounted
to the quarter deck of a tin-plate spooler
larger than a frigate, two of which
fed a factory that took up a city block.
"Never push it," he said. "Breaks all
the circuits, shuts down half the plant."
"It's that big," he answered, "so you
can reach it with your foot or head
if this fucker starts to make a meal of you."

A purple scar ran, like Ahab's, from hairline
to collar and down beneath, souvenir
of a month in ICU, he said, and a year
in rehab after a roller caught his sleeve.
"Leg was a fucking inch too short
to reach the button," he said, rolling
a cigarette with his yellow fingers,
then smoking it down to half an inch.

After a quick review of the counters, dials,
lights, and buttons, he disappeared,
while tin plate, cut into yard-square
pieces, streaked in at 600 feet
a minute, filling the wooden pallet
in front of me till it overflowed and

they piggy backed, then took flight—
heavy, razor sharp—up six feet,
spinning like Ninja throwing stars,
then descending 15 toward
unsuspecting fellow workers. So

I slapped the button, which brought things
to a jolting halt. No one was hit,
but it took four techs two hours
to restart the thing. I expected the boot.

But next day our union steward led me
to another job: putting rows of cans
in rows of boxes—on the night shift.
When I thanked him, he said, "I'm told
to keep members on the payroll, even
dipshits," then walked away.

SPOILAGE

When the can company switched me to working
near the heavy presses, my ears rang all the time,
a high-pitched dial tone. Their doctor said
that was normal, not to expect workman's comp

or time off. The company didn't offer ear plugs,
and we were too stupid or heedless to buy them.
No safety gloves either, for those who had to
handle tinplate that whipped out razor sharp.

One guy took a week to get stitched up,
his hand like a job by Dr. Frankenstein.
They gave us 15-minute breaks twice a day,
but the union steward said, "Don't let me

see your ass back here inside 45." I ate lunch
from the machines: the cafeteria food stank
like soup-kitchen leftovers. An efficiency expert
said to speed the lines way up, which made

some of us go haywire now and then, driving
forklifts into walls, shoving screwdrivers into cogs
that moved the conveyer belts. "Brrrr-*reak*down!"
somebody'd whoop, to a wave of cheers. One day

I shoved a hand truck into a 10-foot stack
of gallon oil cans, watched them crunch in,
topple, and gimp across the floor like busted
wind-up toys: *Havoline Motor . . . Keeps Your*

Engine . . . . Mike Reid, our asshole foreman,
would try to get you fired for stuff like that
or if you worked too slow. But the building
took up half a city block, offering lots of places

out of sight. Anyway, we weren't surprised
to read about some guy showing up to work
one day and shooting every white shirt
he could find. Halfway into my second summer,

the company sent us letters saying they'd had
$100,000 worth of "spoilage" so far that year,
and would we please "help our team get
back on track." Then came another letter,

asking us to consider buying stock, to boost
our "sense of ownership." No shit: "ownership."

REDEYE PINS

We worked clean-up, my older buddy Ed
and I, stuck on the graveyard shift

at Continental Can in Cicero. Twelve years
on the job, Ed shuffled like a lifer circling

the exercise yard. After pushing our brooms
around awhile, sometimes we'd nap

for the last few hours on pallets inside box cars,
when our boss would say, "Don't let me see you

bums again till we clock out," then disappear.
No one else would see us, since the plant,

an antique three-story pile that took up
half a block, was shut down till dawn.

The place reminded me of a flick I saw,
where a neutron bomb went off, leaving

the few survivors on earth to wander
through empty downtown streets. Echoes

mocked them when they yelled to be heard.
The vacant world looked pitiful and useless.

But mostly, we'd go bowling across the street
at All Nite Lanes, where junkies and winos cruised

the lot for spare change. Keeping score
seemed pointless as the rest of what we did,

so we'd just bowl a few frames, slow-like,
refreshed on Buds with vodka chasers.

Other alleys were nearly always empty,
like I was in the doomsday flick again.

One night, we'd just picked out our shoes,
which, even with the foot powder,

smelled like some bum's dirty socks.
When I tried mine on, they felt, for a change,

like they'd been made for me. Amazing.
As we went to bowl, the rental guy yelled,

"Hey, kid, looks like you're startin' to walk
like the rest of us poor motherfuckers."

THE TIN-CAN BOXER

plants the cans clattering side-by-side
along a metal conveyer into 500-can

cardboard boxes. The cans roll in
nonstop like the pies in that skit

about the sap in the pie factory,
pies surging till their neat line goes

kerflooy. The cans flow steadily but
fast as an efficiency expert found

to be just short of what a worker
can stand and not turn liability.

They're boxed in tens with a wooden rake,
boxed until he sees the stream of cans

become a xylophone, which plays
the golden oldies, "Just the Way You Are,"

"Best of My Love," he used to dance to
before he wound up a lifer on the line.

In his latest dream, the xylophone morphed
into a magazine for the fifty-caliber

machine gun he trained on in the Marines,
where the gunny named him "Thumbs."

It cut down a platoon of targets
wearing scowls and white shirts

like the bosses do. But mostly it blurs
into life rolling by, boxed in 12-ounce cans

and hauled away. He's looking for a T-shirt
that says something funny about cans.

BACCALAUREATE

It was at hand: I was about to be anointed
Bachelor of Arts by my state university,
band fanfaring, parents in the stands,
Mom with parasol, Dad in suit and tie,
sun beaming down on the football stadium,

where 3,000 candidates (excluding new MDs
and lawyers, who'd get to come up one by one)
were told to stand and be conferred,
after which even the women were bachelors,
and we sat down, as we were told to.

The valediction, by a greeting-card exec,
("Your future lies before you . . . .")
preceded the call to rise and get our diplomas
at the hot dog stand under the bleachers,
some wag asking for mustard on his

as we lined up before the empty dispensers.
We were issued empty folders, faux leather,
with the school seal stamped in faux gold.
The diplomas, we were told, would arrive
later, in the mail. Mine was in philosophy,

which would require two more degrees
to land a slim chance for a steerage berth
on academia's already-listing liner—
no tenure tracks since Wittgenstein's.
I walked onward, my future before me.

LUCKY THEM

For those who believe in diligence,
earnestness, patience, fairness,
and expertise, consider history.

The Post Office printed an air-mail stamp
with the Jenny biplane upside down,
its holder up a million, then two.

Alexander Fleming, careless with samples,
returned from a two-week holiday
and, in the petri dish—oops—penicillin.

Olympic underdog Steven Bradbury,
won gold when skaters in the lead
all fell, Zambonis for his happy way.

Henry V and company trounced the odds
at Agincourt, when the cocky French
charged into a rain-soaked quagmire.

When some of us who struggle to pay
the bills and get the kids to school,
read about another stupid windfall,

we wonder what came next: maybe
gout, heartbreak, a spot on the x-ray,
or a summons from the I.R.S.

AT MILITARY SCOOL

It was my first teaching job, English comp
to three sections of uniformed rejects, whom
parents didn't want to deal with: slackers,

delinquents, droopy sad sacks. In a school
that looked like a fortress, they were marched
to martial tunes in dress that looked

more student prince than military.
Grades were rigged to humor parents,
who'd find their flunky son had become

a scholar and a gentleman, reviewed
in close-order drill instead of lineups.
On weekends, some got passes to be bussed

in uniform 20 miles to a college town,
where they stood on corners, getting cat calls
from frat boys in convertibles, cold shoulders

instead of dates. There was a suicide,
maybe from the bullying. They graduated
bitter, angry, and good with a gun.

TEACHING SHAKESPEARE
BACK THEN

There they are, at their desks again,
looking much as they did when
mini skirts and sideburns were in style.
There's Paul the Objectivist, repelled by
Hamlet's vacillation. And there she is, my
most devoted student, whose name

I can't recall, and Frank, the brightest,
in his Big Smiths and seed company hat.
"I love Porsches, too," blurted Doug,
when I asked if there were questions.
"It's Portia," I said, "P-o-r-t-i-a."
That's Linda, showing a honeyed thigh.

And, of course, Jasonn-with-two-n's,
the class asshole, who acted as if
we were there to study his postures.
It seems I got issued one of him
every other term. The others are also here,
gray center of the bell curve, whose faces

seem interchangeable. And there I am,
up front, groggy from grading papers
till one a.m., as I try to persuade a few
that Shakespeare isn't just for twits,

stuffed shirts, and English profs—before
Jasonn snags Linda's attention again.
But I had my days when things went right,
and I thank the hoary spires of Academe
for the dear, steadfast what's-her-name.

MAINTENANCE

Today, like yesterday and those before,
I'm taking out the trash. It's wrapped in white

plastic bags with tie-strings, so the trash men
will accept it, those who sometimes rip the tops

off our handy hinged-top cans and chuck them
in the drive. We do not like our work,

those surly men and I. But if we shirked,
the trash would burgeon into monstrous heaps

of stench and staphylococci. So we do
our part in blight control, a role that grows

as we get older; a task the trash men share
with plumbers, firemen, dentists, cops, and surgeons,

who all get better pay. I've squandered half
my life cleaning up infected prose,

taking out cliches, subject-verb
collisions, crippled syllogisms, bloated

verbiage—which I sack in non-judgmental blue,
as damage eats up more and more of life:

there's another spill, a brand new clog,
comma splice, another sore that seeps.

We carry on like Sisyphus, but by and by,
we know, there'll only be those boundless heaps.

THE HARVARD CLASSICS

My grandfather bought a set for his living room,
fifty-one imitation-leather-bound volumes billed

by Collier & Son as a liberal education distilled
to "a five-foot shelf." He was a university dean—

OK, of agriculture—but they looked like something
from bookshelves in films about the highborn,

had that air of seasoned privilege, of green swards,
laced with groundskeepers, footmen, upstairs maids.

When Grandpa died, my father, who didn't read
books, moved them to our living room, said they

showed class, taste, education. The room tried on
their eminence, became a trifle less unHarvard.

One afternoon, intrigued, I pulled out Volume 4,
Complete Poems in English, Milton, whose sermonics

in thundering blank verse dismissed me back
to my shelf of *Classic Comics.* Ten years later,

the books languished in a yard sale, marked down
with their kind in yards across the country.

COMMITTEE MEETING

A beating with nettle-
coated noodles,

mind entreating fight
or stealthy fleeing

the depleting kit
and dull caboodle. I doodle

cartoon faces and bouquets
of loopy squiggles

as time drags along,
excreting mustard gas.

Is this the will's unseating
as seeming centuries

creep by like slugs
retreating over salt? Is there

no halt to this browbeating,
where hot air keeps on

competing with itself
for front-row seating

de-meating issues
down to bare-boned blather,

meting out *ennui*
as pores keep leaking

in this overheating
of the stomach's juices

that makes us strain
to keep our bowels

from blowing bubbles
(O toil and trouble!) while buffs

redouble notions they won't
even start completing,

and pain comes fullback-
cleating up our spines

in this Lilliputian strudel,
repeating and repeating,

eating up the years
till flying sheep send down

their bleatings and chickadees
go moo instead of tweeting?

AFTER SURPRISING CONVERSIONS

They're aired between evening TV
sound bites of homicides, suicides,
fratricides, infanticides, fires, floods,

and pols. Befores, pajamaed or in undies,
look old and lonely in their ills, one
with a headache big as her living room.

They buckle with pain, sneeze and cough
staccato, rush to the toilet, nod off
at their desks, snap at their worried spouses.

Afters jog together at Big Sur, cavort
with their now-adoring grandkids. Mates
hold hands in twin bathtubs, renewed

and busy at their sponsor-vetted
foreplay. A former-wetter guffaws
worry-free at the Improv, while side-effects—

dizziness, rash, fever, constipation,
incontinence, delusions. thrombosis, stroke—
await, all snickers and high-fives.

CASH COW

No stupid moo-cow or piggy-bank sow for loose change
   and pocket lint, or sacred cow you've got to kowtow to.
     Not a bell cow to lead you down some lumpy cow path fraught
       with cow pies or maybe down you with a dose of cow pox or lure

      some lonely cowpoke through a shitload of choke-weed. No, not even
     how now's brown cow—but a gen-u-ine Cash Cow that gulps
   down overdrafts, bills, and IOUs, and gives crisp Jeffersons, Grants,
and Franklins—plus municipals, treasuries, corporates, stocks,

and debentures. Such bovine bounty: *Mince alors!* Who'd trade that
   for a handful of magic beans, much less a hill of them? Anyhow, my cow
     gets me mooney as Ron Popeil dreaming the Veg-O-Matic, glows
       holy as a rosette of sawbucks. I stash my cash in a Scrooge-McDuck-

      sized corn crib, were I cavort splish-splash porpoise-like before
     time out for a foamy brew or two. Don't dis me if I miss the news,
   watching that lucre accrue from my moolah-maker, which keeps
ticking new booty even when it takes a licking. To all whose ear

is near or nearly so: Don't grouse to me about the arid lips
   of penury. As my daddy, who had the Cash Cow knowhow, would
     shout: One in the hand beats two in Muncie. To that I'd add
       the utterance of Howdy Doody's unstrung bud Chief Thunderthud:

      Cowabunga!

WHY WAIT?

—car dealer ad

Waiting on hold since before Marconi,
waiting for my slice of humble pie to cool,
waiting for the acid test results,
waiting for a nod from slumber's border guard,
waiting for the black hole to learn decent table manners,
waiting for the bloodstains to come clean,
waiting for a member discount,
waiting for inspiration's yodel,
waiting for my portfolio to gel,
waiting for a price check,
waiting for minty-fresh breath,
waiting for touchdown on my choppy flight across the week,
waiting for dumb luck to flounder in,
waiting for the heebie jeebies to observe the
     Marquess of Queensberry rules,
waiting for customer service to send a decent
     translation of the user's guide,
waiting for a jump start on the road to recovery,
waiting for the music of the spheres to take requests.

SONG OF THE BLACK HOLE

(radially extracted by NASA)

You can almost see Vincent Price, black-robed,
hunched above the console of a jumbo organ
in the bowels of his creaky haunted manse; or
maybe a stadium of damned souls, strobed
in lurid red and howling nettle-robed
as they plummet into Pandemonium, pore
and pith aflame. It's no troubadour,
undoubtedly, this vast atonal gob.

As with the Roach Motel, we'd check in,
but never out—us or anything, since
it can swallow errant planets whole and still,
however much the mass, can't eat its fill.
Though it's larger far than Jupiter or Mars,
we can barely see it, thank our lucky stars.

III

VOYAGE TO OUTER SPACE

It used to fire up the imagination:
Trip to the Moon, Flash Gordon,
Star Trek, 2001: a Space Odyssey.

But after Armstrong's "one small step,"
it's begun to look as if we're surrounded
by billions of vacant lots: the moon,

the nine planets, and, Webb Telescope
notwithstanding, the cosmos, barren
as that acreage in the old Florida real-estate

scam. Who would want to settle on
one of those year-round-hostile outbacks?
We do, developers say. Already, there's talk

of lunar hotels and anti-drift tethers
for zero-gravity sex. But maybe those lots
weren't always vacant. Maybe their inhabitants

did to their planet what we're doing to ours.
Maybe they've left a trail of mayhem
throughout the galaxy. Maybe we're them.

A SECOND LOOK
AT BRUEGEL'S *THE TOWER OF BABEL*

Tiny detail down on the right-hand side,
a worker stands before a brace of oxen
near the shore. He looks away from the pride
of Shinar, which juts through a wispy shock
of cloud. Faced toward ships that bring the stones,
bricks, and timber, he leans slightly forward,
resting, maybe letting out a sigh,
before the grind begins again. Unstirred,
he's left the zeal at hand to those who've
ordered it and shaped his pinched existence.
Six huge stacks of bricks loom
as he stands there gazing seaward. Witness
to the lunatic upheaval, his wages known,
he'll leave Nimrod and his toadies to their own.

ON BRUEGEL'S
MASSACRE OF THE INNOCENTS

He's switched the scene from Bethlehem
to 16th-century Flanders, from Herod's rampage

to the Spanish Duke of Alba's. Had he lived longer,
it could have been Wounded Knee, Babi Yar,

My Lai, or someplace we've yet to hear of.
Bunched soldiers block the road out of town.

In front of them, the butchery unfolds, children
skewered before their begging parents, more

bleeding-out on the snow. In the foreground,
assailants batter down a door, as others

climb through a window. Four more
circle in, spearing infants one by one

as a woman sits on the ground, baby sprawled
in her lap, and a straggler trots by, hunting

for his first. From a distance, captains observe
the show, bet if it will end in time for lunch.

DULCE ET DECORUM

(Statue at the Shot at Dawn Memorial,
Staffordshire, UK)

He stands there, larger than he could have been
in life: Private Herbert Burden, Northumberland

Fusiliers, who lied about his age
to join the Great War, shot at 17

to scare the others into staying put.
Cast in whitish stone, blindfold on,

hands bound, boyish mop uncombed,
trench coat open, a disc to mark his heart,

he waits before 300 posts that stand
for others, privates almost all, who shared

his fall-guy luck among 3,000 whose deaths
were never carried out. Pardoned with the rest

in 2006, he stands up straight and still,
as he was taught, holding his stone breath.

STILL LIFE

(near Srebrenica, 1998)

It took dominion everywhere.
        —Stevens, "Anecdote of the Jar"

A shoe stands
at the forest edge,

tongue depressed
with spectacles

and one gray sock.
It's quiet now:

no more cries
and volleys.

A breeze ripples
the maple leaves,

cicadas chirr,
the sky's bright blue—

all poised in place
around the shoe.

CONTAGION

Let's hope we don't catch it. I'd hate to wake up
some morning and find out that you weren't you.
　　　　　　—Invasion of the Body Snatchers

Some squares are really circles, Daddy said.
They're round inside but hide it cleverly—
a snaky trait, and maybe it could spread.

They have no point so might as well be dead.
Alive they put us all in jeopardy:
those squares are circled round us, Daddy said.

It clearly has to do with how they're bred,
not like us, who do with qualms and brevity
that seamy act whose germs they're known to spread.

What makes them act that way we dread
to talk about, it shakes our poise so readily.
Some squares would make us circles, Daddy said.

We'd like to take them to the backyard shed
and whip them till their backside's leathery.
And hesitating only helps it spread.

The slippery slope they hope to have us sled
we fear as much as death or even bankruptcy.
Some squares are really circles, Daddy said,
and feeling round some nights, we fear it's spread.

MERCY

(found poem based on 1998 Interview of a Lithuanian
rifleman in Einsatzgruppen B from 1939-45)

Nobody told us what our duties would be.

They just trucked us in one morning.

We only knew our destination when we got there.

It was a military secret.

It was some little town.

I forgot its name.

All the Jewish men were off at war.

Only old folks, women, and children remained.

They were the people we were ordered to kill.

It was shoot or be shot.

The gunners were side by side along the pit with
    the Jews in it.

We didn't shoot the Jews on the edges.

We killed them after they were forced to lie down
     in it.

We shot the adults first, then the children—
     so the parents wouldn't have to see their children die.

They were brave.

They never screamed or begged.

They lay down, ready to die.

They all had the Star of David on their backs.

To avoid being beaten, they didn't resist.

We'd shoot the nearest victim.

We barely moved the rifle, the person was so close.

 We fired two or three bullets.

We tried to aim accurately.

One Jewish man pointed to his chest so we'd aim
     at it.

I shot him there.

If I'd have only wounded him, he'd have suffocated
     under the others.

We had to shoot the children dead, or they'd have
    died by suffocation.

We used incendiary bullets.

They burnt the clothes.

The burnt smell was everywhere.

The older children knew their fate.

They lay down in the pit.

The little ones tried to crawl over to their dead
    parents.

They crawled on all fours.

The Germans kept the pits surrounded.

They didn't shoot: they supervised.

The Lithuanian soldiers had to shoot the Jews.

German soldiers took photos.

After the execution, German officers walked on
    the bodies and used their pistols to shoot the
    people still alive.

The Germans brought POWs from the camps
  nearby.

The POWs poured disinfectant on the bodies and
  shoveled earth over them.

Someone asked what I'd say now to a child whose
  parents I killed.

I don't know.

The little ones . . . .

I'd say, "there there."

THE ONES WHO'D
CARRY IT OUT

Some may live just a block away,
even nearer: the Walmart clerk
who'd cooly hook a hot wire
to your gonads, the grease monkey
keen on beheading, the cleaning lady
who'd fill her pail with eyeballs.

There's the ousted Scoutmaster
who'd corral the kids, the engineer
who'd craft a more cost-effective
abattoir for undesirables, the MBA
who'd plot the sweeping purges
and drive the schedule full tilt.

Add to them, the rubberneckers,
who'd only want a decent view—
and those, like most, who'd say
the acrid smoke billowing from
that odd new building's chimney
is simply none of their affair.

ARCHAEOPTERYX

One of evolution's also-rans, it got
stuck with a moniker that presaged
drug company concoctions ("Life's
got you down? Try Archaeopteryx.")

It had feathers jammed into a lizard
body, it's "flight" a flapping hop,
claws ill-suited for perching safely above
its predators, if it could have flown there.

Glitz ridden as the Edsel, it was doomed
to disappear. And if the earth survives
our goose step, cash flow, and glacier
liquidation, we may end up asleep

in shale with the archaeopteryx:
discarded lemons, fossilized.

LITTLE-KNOWN
ROYAL COGNOMENS

Consider Bruno of Campania,
The Laughing Nipple,

thought a misreading
of "The Lord of Naples,"

and Hubert The Shit-and-Flee
of Wessex, named for his battle

tactics, and Bernard of Silesia,
called The Lonely Gonad

following his near-fatal duel
with Rudolph of Bavaria,

The Winged Parsnip, a tag
of uncertain origin. Then

there's Ragnar of Kalunborg,
The Filled-with-Edam,

in reference to the only
Norse attempt to mummify,

and Stephan of Provence,
deemed The Reeking Flyspeck

by the conquering Armin of Saxony,
then proclaimed Mightier-

Than-The-Flyspeck. Also noteworthy,
Andre of Toulouse, whose queen,

Simone, The Festooned Eggplant,
dubbed him The Tower

of Nose Hair. Finally, we have
The Lousy Murdering

Dung-Brained Bastard
Whom Everybody

Halfway Sane Wants
To See Eaten By Dogs,

a title too widespread
for sole attribution.

VIVA VILLA

The jury's in, summoned
by Villa: six peons, cut down
from nearby trees, still
wearing their nooses.

They stare in all directions
as he asks if any
objects to the execution
of the *hacendados*
and their cronies quivering
behind the witness stand.

The dead's silence
fills the room
with the indifference
their misery met with
from the condemned.
Villa asks again,
even more politely,
if there are any objections.

OK, this was only
an old film, starring
Wallace Beery as yet
another Robin Hood
dreamed up to distract us

from an even older
verdict the *hacendados*
know is in their favor.
But bless our dreams,
bless the silent peons,
and viva Villa.

IV

DOUBTERS GATE

*[Heaven] had a wall great and high, and had
twelve gates, and at the gates twelve angels.*

—Revelation 21:12

At the turnstile, you face the angel Wendell.
He wants you to provide a photo I.D.,

your dental history, and $49.99 in fees.
He's typing his report on an old Smith Corona.

In the distance, there's what sounds like
a barbershop quartet on helium.

He acts hurried, which makes him sometimes
hit the wrong keys, which he takes out on you

by deliberately mispronouncing your name
in a voice that sounds like Liberace's.

He says all the gnashing's gotten to him,
that he's going back into bliss therapy,

then hands you the typewriter and disappears.
When you look behind, the line seems to reach

the horizon. "Next!" your mouth says.
It feels right, as if you've always been here.

ON RESURRECTION

You join your family and old friends,
whom you're glad to find restored. Alas,
there's also old Miss Harper whose Bible class
gave you a stiff dose of world without end.
There's the fifth-grade bully, who owned recess
and your high-school football coach, still
in cleats, whom you thought would be in hell
with Hitler, Himmler, Goebbels, and the rest.

Everyone who helped to change your dance
from "The Cha Cha" to "The Turtle" crowd
in on you, including swarms of ants,
mosquitoes, gnats, and mantises you sprayed,
whom decades later still recall that snouted
devil with its goddamned can of Raid.

LAMENT FOR
THE HOT RODS

their spectrum of shapes
and fuck-you roars,

their Frenched headlights,
their Holley quads,

and Naugahyde;
their low-slung frames

sculpted for speed,
their sashay ways:

'32 Deuce, '50 Merc,
'68 Mustang,

candy-apple red,
electric blue,

metallic heliotrope,
Isky-cammed,

Positractioned,
chopped, channeled,

Von Dutch striped;
    revving at stoplights,

staged for the sprint
    with scream of tires,

and the nightly cruise.
    Now it's the pickups,

alike as clones,
    bloated, oafish,

everywhere.

FRIEND IN A BOX

What's left of him, that is,
six feet four sealed in mahogany
eight inches by twelve, carried in
for the funeral reception, placed

on a table, unnoticed by most,
nearly by me. College buddies
sixty years ago, we still
met now and then, chatting

about fraternity days—their echoes
of *Animal House*—our latest ailments,
the Royals and Chiefs, the nation's
slapstick woes. A storm of illnesses

brought him here, where at first,
I thought the box to be some
ill-advised gift for his widow.
Leaving, I felt an urge to ask him

how it is in there. Given voice,
he'd have told me, "You'll
find out." My other friends
in urns and boxes would agree.

LOST

Did your Safeway turn foreign as Madrid
when they shifted things around, Aisle Three
for Aisle Five, canned veggies for bread,
salt for vinegar—because ad men agree
we'll buy more, as if to bribe our way
back across the border to the known?
In childhood, ever lose sight of Mother, say
in Cereals, panic flashing through your bones—
the grins of Snap, Crackle, even Pop
gone cold till some kind hand led you back
from orphanhood? Could this foretell a stop
when the drive to work, a walk around the block
or to the bathroom for an urgent pee
bewilders like a labyrinth? We'll see.

WORSE THAN USELESS

Maybe you said that about a piece of crap
you bought online or what advertised itself
as "customer service." Maybe a coach
said it when you missed an easy tackle

or some boss muttered it on your first day,
when you cooked the curly fries too long.
Maybe you even said it to yourself, though
you didn't really mean it, not then anyway.

But what about those stored in "total care"
facilities, named for dying things or seasons:
sunset, autumn, golden fields; or for fantasies
like Bel-air Manor and Sunshine Vista. What

can their inmates call themselves, nodding off
or watching out their solitary window,
which overlooks the parking lot, hoping
to spot someone they know or maybe just

a cardinal or finch flitting by, instead of
the scrounging sparrows, all of whom still
have some function in the scheme of things?
The body's built to atrophy. Its organs clog

or slowly peter out, despite the ads that make
believe it can't be true. Lay up your poison pills,
your .45, before you can't remember where
to get them or which orifice to put them in.

Make yourself useful.

ABOARD THE AUTUMN HOUSE
"OATS EXPRESS"

Confined in that aqua minibus, they seldom
feel their oats, much less sow wild ones. They feel
the urge to venture from their soured rooms
in the "home" some may have joked about. They'll
shop some mall or watch a matinee,
the air no longer tinged with Lysoled dread
or daily warbles for "Nurse," or "Momma," or
maybe a metronomic "Help me." They've forfeited
their cars and houses. Their favorite food and drink
play havoc with their bowels and don't taste right.
Their knees, hips, and memories are on the blink,
their spunk spent. But these riders stay polite
and sympathetic, smile instead of stew.
Live long enough, they'll save a seat for you.

RADIATION DAY

We sit together in a hallway once a week,
old guys wearing sweat pants for easy
dropping when its time for our ten minutes
under the ray aimed at our prostates.

I wore sweats on my high school track team,
when we warmed up for a meet—far cry
from the high-class duds that adorned
the basketball team, who got cheerleaders, too.

The doctor told us we'd need a full bladder
for the burn to work right. If the drive home's
too far, some often have to pull off
to unleash in a cup. Mine's an ex Big Gulp.

We must make this run forty-three times,
after which the nurses will ring a bell
and give us a cheer for outpacing death,
striding patiently somewhere behind.

Distance runs, the mile for instance,
require several laps around the track.
An official sounds the onset of the final one,
called "the bell lap."

AT LONG LAST!

Users of this miracle
E.D. cure may experience
the following side effects:

headaches, dizziness,
nausea, hives, diarrhea,
sleep apnea, partial paralysis,

homicidal impulses, projectile
vomiting, pink elephants, priapism,
St. Vitus Dance, demonic possession,

drooling idiocy, visions of sugarplums,
earworm of Yanni's greatest hits, elephantiasis,
sudden death, which can worsen balance problems,

increased risk of spontaneous detonation,
    acquisition
of phony French accent, sudsoriattaphobia (fear of
    soap-on-a-rope),
googly eyes, rectal yodeling, and/or the condition
    known as "traveling penis."

For complete list of side effects,
see accompanying booklet.

FAMILY ALBUM

It's from the '40s, the black-and-white photos
held fast at the corners with little black tabs:
me in my diapers, me on my wooden pony,
me in my father's arms, dwarfed under
his service cap, me in my starched sailor suit.
Beneath each photo, my sister, twelve years
older, noted the occasion in her precocious
script. There are no photos of my mother,
probably down with her depression.
No one else was there to keep a record
of little brother—Mother ill, Dad off at war—
only my sister with her pen and Kodak Brownie.

Now, we just trade Christmas gifts
and birthday cards. I have no memory of
her devotion back then, only the album,
with those meticulous notations, fine-point
white on the black pages, stored in a box
shelved somewhere in the basement.

POST MORTEM
February 3, 1959

You might not see the bodies in the famous photo
of the Cessna wadded against a farm fence,

first responders standing, arms down,
in the fresh snow. But in another,

the flattened white figure ten feet away
was Buddy Holly, Ritchie Valens' remains

sprawled a few yards east. The Bopper's
barely visible, jettisoned some 40 feet

beyond the fence. You wouldn't want to see
any closer. The coroner's report mentions

"spongy" chests, missing brain matter,
the plane having hit the ground at around

170 miles an hour and rolling 500 feet
or so into a ball, flinging out bodies

before it hit the fence, pilot inside.
A Caddy ambulance, idling, stares ahead.

I was a high school senior then. I don't
know why I'm telling you all this.

SIX TO TEN INCHES

It's slanting from the north in soggy puffs,
now blanketing the drive in leaden berms,
what our Cheshire-grinning weather man has termed
"a dandy." So I'm out in coat, gloves, and muffs
face chilled, moustache frosting up,
shoveling with my pensioned kind, some
of whose plaque-encrusted hearts may start to drum
retreat as their lives clatter in Fate's dice cup.

I could hire the neighbor kids, now working fast
and stroke-proof down the street, who'd get by
on fifteen bucks. But we must stay steadfast,
our grizzled corps, senior Sisyphi
who wheeze and sweat on death's trap door,
aiming to show the bloody gods what for.

PORPHYRION

(Image from the Low-Frequency Array
Radio Telescope)

The rays, flashed from both sides
of a black hole, with conflagrations
at each end, are twenty-three million
light years long, with an energy level
equal to the output of a trillion stars
and wide as a hundred-forty Milky Ways.

It's in a galaxy seven-point five billion
light years from here, which means
what we're seeing now is eons in the past,
when the universe was less than half
the current age of fourteen billion years
and we were wafting space dust.

Maybe it's petered out, though there's
likely space for millions more, any
of which could vaporize earth, making
us on our "big" blue marble seem less
than dust mites on a styrofoam peanut,
minus a trillion sizes or two.

But we've got Stravinsky, Mozart, Bach,
and, rocking up there with the rest,
Berry, whom we blasted aboard
Voyager into the vast indifference. "Go,"
we belt out in our heartiest yawp,
"Go, Johnny, Go!"

MOON

For the first time it met my eyes as a globe.
The word "moon" came into my mouth
as though fed to me out of a spoon. Held
in my mouth, the moon became a word.
　　　　—Eudora Welty, *One Writer's Beginnings*

So there, post-modernists, the word
has meaning, which we depend on,
like when the coolest sticker you
could put on your hotrod was "Moon
Equipped." It's why we favor moon
roofs or get all moony over love,

in hand or lost. We see a man in it,
or woman, entrancing, who seems to
smile or, other times, scowl and say
"Oh no" when Jackie Gleason barks,
"One-a dese days, Alice: Pow!
Ta da moon!" or when the latest wag

moons the stands or when someone
claims it's all green cheese. It's why
Neil Armstrong let us down, when,
muffing his declaration, he stepped
onto that talcum wasteland many said
was in some studio backlot. Our moon

is more like Melies', grimacing when
the spaceship pokes into his eye. It's why
that young man "never saw the sixpence
lying at his feet." It's what wolves howl at
and what made a wolf man out of poor
Larry Talbot. It makes waves, literally

in the ocean, and in our blood, is what
we shoot for when we bet it all. Moon
Over Miami, Moon River, Moon Shadow,
Blue Moon, That Old Devil Moon,
Fly Me to the Moon—yes, O word de-
(con) structonists, Moon, Moon, Moon!

HOT SPELL

Heat index of 120, humidity past
Sumatra's, our truthie congressman
says, "It's just summer, stupid."

Even our dog, tongue hanging out
above an air vent, knows better.
Our AC's hit DEFCON 2. Power

& Light's hiring more lawyers. It's worse
in Phoenix, where falling on asphalt
causes third-degree burns. Armageddon

films and games are in, as are
survival kits, Tasers, and assault rifles.
Hotel chains plan for a bidding war

to grab the choicest lots on the moon,
where guest beds may require tethers
for safe sex in zero gravity. TV

offers drug commercials, *Survivor,*
and *American Ninja Warrior,* as end-
timers bellow I-told-you-sos. Still,

the cicadas haven't called it quits,
and our dog's cooled off enough for a nap
beneath the kitchen table as my wife

and I, sharing some 4-power Panang
with a bottle of decent Cab, salute
the audacious chirr outside.

Maintenance is **William Trowbridge's** 11th poetry collection. He has published over 550 poems in literary periodicals and has given readings, lectures, and workshops at schools, universities, bookstores, and literary conferences throughout the United States. His awards include an Academy of American Poets Prize, a Pushcart Prize, a Bread Loaf Writers' Conference scholarship, a Camber Press Poetry Chapbook Award, and fellowships from The MacDowell Colony, Ragdale, Yaddo, and The Anderson Center. He is a Distinguished University Professor Emeritus at Northwest Missouri State University, where he was an editor of *The Laurel Review/GreenTower Press* from 1986 to 2004. He was Poet Laureate of Missouri from 2012 to 2016. He is currently a faculty mentor in the University of Nebraska-Omaha Low-residency MFA in Writing Program. For more information, see his website at williamtrowbridge.net.

This project was made possible, in part, by generous support from the Osage Arts Community.

Osage Arts Community provides temporary time, space and support for the creation of new artistic works in a retreat format, serving creative people of all kinds — visual artists, composers, poets, fiction and nonfiction writers. Located on a 152-acre farm in an isolated rural mountainside setting in Central Missouri and bordered by ¾ of a mile of the Gasconade River, OAC provides residencies to those working alone, as well as welcoming collaborative teams, offering living space and workspace in a country environment to emerging and mid-career artists. For more information, visit us at www.osageac.org

Osage Arts Community

www.ingramcontent.com/pod-product-compliance
Lightning Source LLC
Chambersburg PA
CBHW021121130626
46554CB00002B/800